The Life and Work of...

Barbara Hepworth

Jayne Woodhouse

Heinemann
LIBRARY

H www.heinemann.co.uk/library
Visit our website to find out more information about Heinemann Library books.

To order:
☎ Phone 44 (0) 1865 888066
▤ Send a fax to 44 (0) 1865 314091
▢ Visit the Heinemann Bookshop at www.heinemann.co.uk/library to browse our catalogue and order online.

First published in Great Britain by Heinemann Library, Halley Court, Jordan Hill, Oxford OX2 8EJ, a division of Reed Educational and Professional Publishing Ltd. Heinemann is a registered trademark of Reed Educational & Professional Publishing Ltd.

OXFORD MELBOURNE AUCKLAND JOHANNESBURG BLANTYRE
GABORONE IBADAN PORTSMOUTH (NH) USA CHICAGO

© Reed Educational and Professional Publishing Ltd 2002
The moral right of the proprietor has been asserted.

Designed by Celia Floyd
Originated by Ambassador Litho Ltd
Printed and bound in Hong Kong/China

ISBN 0 431 09212 5 (hardback)   ISBN 0 431 09215 X (paperback)

06 05 04 03   06 05 04 03
10 9 8 7 6 5 4 3 2   10 9 8 7 6 5 4 3 2

British Library Cataloguing in Publication Data

Woodhouse, Jayne
  The life and work of Barbara Hepworth
  1. Hepworth, Barbara, 1903-1975
  2. Women sculptors –- England – Biography – Juvenile literature
  3. Sculptors – England – Biography – Juvenile literature
  4. Sculpture – England – Juvenile literature
  I. Title   II. Barbara Hepworth
  730.9'2

Acknowledgements
The Publisher would like to thank the following for permission to reproduce photographs: Alan Bowness, Hepworth Estate: pp4, 10, 13, 22, 23, 24, 27; Andrew Besley: p28; Bridgeman Art Library: p9; Hulton Getty: pp8, 14; John Cleare Mountain Photography: p6; Popperfoto: p26; Robert Harding Picture Library: p18; Science Photo Library: p20; Scottish National Gallery of Modern Art: p5; Tate Archive: pp12, 16; Tate Gallery, St Ives: p29; Tate Picture Library: pp7, 11, 15, 17, 19, 21, 25.

Cover photograph: *Merryn,* Barbara Hepworth, 1962 (alabaster, 13 x 11½ x 8¼ in.), gift of Wallace and Wilhelmina Holladay. Reproduced with permission of the National Museum of Women in the Arts.

All Hepworth works of art copyright © Alan Bowness, Hepworth Estate.

Every effort has been made to contact copyright holders of any material reproduced in this book. Any omissions will be rectified in subsequent printings if notice is given to the Publisher.

Any words appearing in the text in bold, **like this**, are explained in the Glossary.

Contents

Who was Barbara Hepworth?   4

Early years   6

Learning to be an artist   8

Motherhood   10

Changing ideas   12

A new family   14

Working life   16

St Ives   18

Different ways of working   20

Large forms   22

New materials   24

Fame and honours   26

A tragic end   28

Timeline   30

Glossary   31

More books to read, sculptures to see
and websites   31

Index   32

Who was Barbara Hepworth?

Barbara Hepworth was one of the great modern artists to come from the UK. She was a famous **sculptor**. In Barbara's time, this was a very unusual thing for a woman to be.

Barbara's most important **sculptures** are **abstract art**. They are made from wood, stone and, later, **bronze**. Barbara said her work was a way of 'holding a beautiful thought'.

Wave, 1943–44

Early years

Barbara was born in Wakefield, Yorkshire, on 10 January 1903. Some of her earliest memories were of the countryside there. She never forgot the shapes made by the roads, hills and fields.

All her life, Barbara was **inspired** by nature and the **landscape**. She made this **bronze sculpture** in 1958, when she lived by the sea. It shows how she saw the waves breaking on the beach.

Sea Form (Porthmeor), 1958

Learning to be an artist

When Barbara was only 17, she went to Leeds School of Art. There she met the **sculptor Henry Moore**, who shared many of her ideas. One year later, Barbara entered the Royal College of Art in London.

Barbara first learnt to **carve** in stone during a visit to Italy in 1924. Her early works were simple figures of people, animals and birds, like this pair of doves.

Doves, 1927

Motherhood

While she was in Italy, Barbara married John Skeaping. He was another British **sculptor**. They returned to London in 1926. Three years later, their son Paul was born.

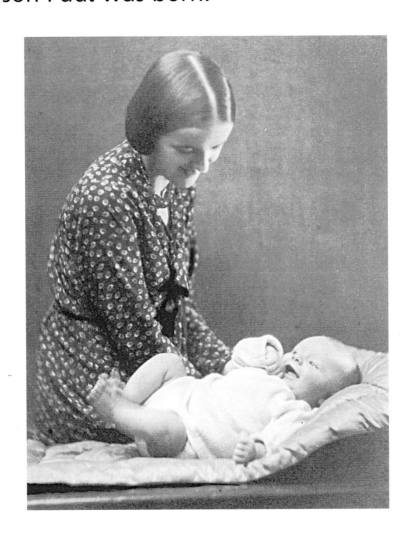

While the baby lay in his cot or on a rug nearby, Barbara would go on with her **carving**. She made this figure of Paul sleeping out of hard, dark wood.

Infant,
1929

11

Changing ideas

From 1930, Barbara began to explore **abstract art**. Her **sculptures** no longer looked like things in real life. Instead, they showed her ideas about shape and space.

This piece of work is called *Pierced Form*. Barbara was one of the first artists to **carve** holes right through the stone. She used this idea many times.

Pierced Form, 1931

13

A new family

In 1931, Barbara met the **abstract** painter Ben Nicholson. He became her second husband. In 1934, Barbara gave birth to **triplets**.

The arrival of her three babies gave Barbara new ideas. She began to make pieces of work in groups of three. This one is **carved** from white **marble**.

Three Forms, 1935

Working life

It was not always easy for Babara to be an artist and a mother. She often had very little time to work. Her **studio** was sometimes a jumble of rocks, **sculptures**, children and washing!

However, Barbara said that her children were always an important **inspiration** to her. In the 1930s, she made several works based on the idea of a mother and child.

Mother and Child, 1934

St Ives

When World War II began in 1939, Barbara and her family moved from London to St Ives in Cornwall. Barbara loved the Cornish **landscape** with its rocky cliffs, sea and bright light.

Barbara called this piece *Pelagos*, which is the Greek word for the sea. It was **inspired** by the view of the land and the waves from her **studio** window. It is made of partly-painted wood and strings.

Pelagos, 1946

Different ways of working

Paintings and drawings were also part of Barbara's work. In the 1940s, Barbara made several visits to hospitals. There she watched operations being carried out.

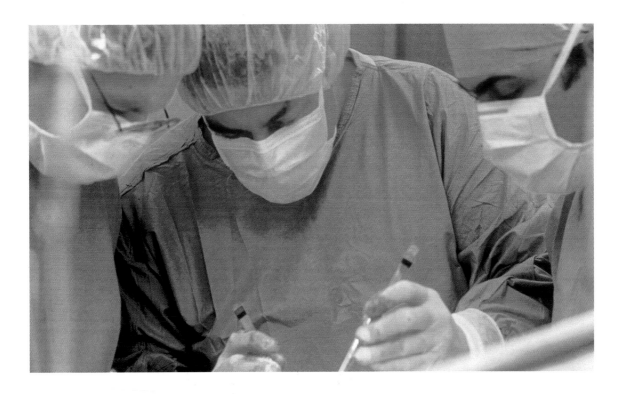

The Scalpel 2, 1949

This drawing is based on **sketches** Barbara made in a hospital **operating theatre**. To Barbara, the way the doctors and nurses worked together seemed like a kind of **sculpture**.

21

Large forms

In 1949, Barbara bought Trewyn **Studio** in St Ives. She lived there for the rest of her life. For the first time she had enough space to make really large **sculptures**.

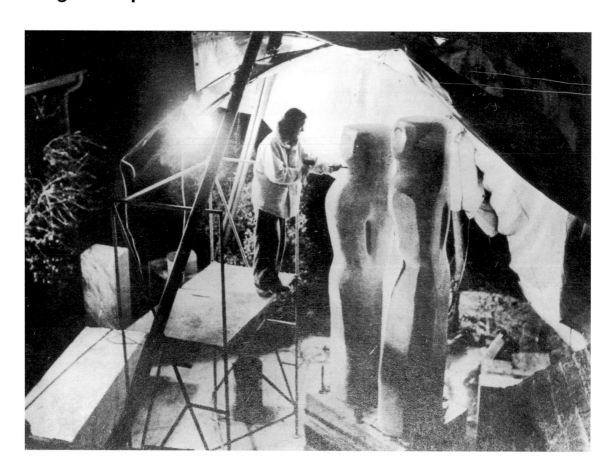

Some of Barbara's large pieces of work were based on human figures. They were made to be seen outside, as part of the **landscape**, not in an art **gallery**.

Contrapuntal Forms, 1951

23

New materials

From the 1950s, Barbara began to work in **bronze**. First she made the sculpture in plaster. Then a **mould** was made of it, into which she poured hot bronze.

This finished **sculpture** is called *Four-Square (Walk Through)*. It is over 4 metres high. Barbara made it for people to walk on and climb through.

Four-Square (Walk Through), 1966

25

Fame and honours

From the 1950s, Barbara became more famous. In 1965 she received an important honour from the Queen. From then on, she was known as Dame Barbara Hepworth. Here she is on the right, with her daughters.

Single Form, 1962–63

Barbara was given many special **commissions**. Her **sculptures** were put in public places where people could see them every day. This one is outside the United Nations building in New York, USA.

A tragic end

Sadly, Barbara died in a fire at her **studio** on 20 May 1975. She was 72 years old. She is buried in St Ives, and this **sculpture** stands nearby.

The following year, the Barbara Hepworth Museum and Sculpture Garden was opened at her old studio. Today, you can visit the place where Barbara worked. You can see many of her sculptures, just as she wished.

Barbara Hepworth Museum and Sculpture Garden

Timeline

1903	Barbara Hepworth is born in Wakefield, Yorkshire on 10 January.
1914	Barbara attends Wakefield Girls' High School.
1914–18	World War I.
1920	Barbara attends Leeds School of Art.
1921	She enters the Royal College of Art, London.
1924	She visits Italy, where she learns to **carve** in stone.
1925	Barbara marries John Skeaping while in Italy.
1926	Barbara and John return to London and set up **studios** there.
1928	Barbara holds her first joint **exhibition** with John.
1929	Her son, Paul, is born.
1931	Barbara meets Ben Nicholson, who later becomes her second husband.
1934	She gives birth to **triplets**.
1939	World War II begins. Barbara moves to St Ives in Cornwall.
1945	World War II ends.
1949	Barbara buys Trewyn Studio in St Ives.
1950s	She has exhibitions in New York, Venice and London.
1965	She is made 'Dame Barbara Hepworth' by the Queen.
1975	Barbara dies in a fire in her studio on 20 May.
1976	The Barbara Hepworth Museum and Sculpture Garden is opened in her old studio.

Glossary

abstract art art that tries to show ideas rather than the way things look

bronze a type of metal

carve cut into a shape

commission being asked to make a piece of art

exhibition public showing of art

gallery room or building where works of art are shown

Henry Moore famous British sculptor born in 1898

inspire to give ideas to

landscape the countryside

marble a type of stone which can be carved and polished

mould a hollow shape for making jellies as well as sculpture

operating theatre room in a hospital where operations are carried out

sculptor artist who works in stone, wood, clay or other materials

sculpture work of art made of stone, wood or other materials

sketch drawing an artist does quite quickly

studio room or building where an artist works

triplets three children born at the same time

More books to read

Famous Lives: Artists, Jillian Powell, Hodder Wayland

How Artists Use Pattern and Texture, Paul Flux, Heinemann Library

Websites

www.tate.org.uk/stives/hepworth

More sculptures to see

Kneeling Figure, Barbara Hepworth, Wakefield City Art Gallery, Wakefield

Winged Figure, Barbara Hepworth, John Lewis Dept Store, Oxford St, London

Index

abstract art   5, 12, 14

birth   6

bronze   5, 7, 24

children   10, 11, 14, 15, 16, 17

Dame Barbara   26

death   28

hospital   20, 21

Italy   9, 10

marriage   10, 14

Moore, Henry   8

St Ives   18, 22, 28

stone   5, 9, 13

studios   16, 19, 22, 28, 29

wood   5, 11, 19

World War II   18